This isn't my traditional Valentine's Day gift (sometimes tradition needs to be put aside), however, I hope the enclosed writings will strike a chord, rekindle a flame, and resound from the highest mountains to the depths of the heart.

joe

God's Word says that, "Love is patient, kind and understanding." He also gives us instructions to follow ei Ephesians 5. Likewise I'm striving to follow Deuteronomy 6:18 (re: obedience unto the Lord). I know He keeps His promises and grant peace to all who obey his will. On today 2/14/02 what could be more fitting to remember that He said "the greatest gift is love."

Peggi

Published by Barbour Publishing, Inc., P.O. Box 719, Uhrichsville, Ohio 44683 www.barbourbooks.com

 Member of the
Evangelical Christian
Publishers Association

Printed in China.

Happy Valentine's Day

Ellyn Sanna

BARBOUR
PUBLISHING, INC.

Life would be a poor, dry thing without love.
That's why I want to say thank you for all the love
you've spread into my life.
And in return, on Valentine's Day—
and always—
I pray that your heart will be rich and overflowing
with all the bounty love has to offer.

. . .love be yours in abundance.

JUDE 1:2 NIV

Contents

One

Love Is Joy

How we thank God for you!
Because of you we have great joy
in the presence of God.

1 THESSALONIANS 3:9 NLT

*D*o you now how often you brighten my life? All the thoughtful things you've done for me make my life a lighter, better place to be. I appreciate you, and I am so thankful.

Most of all, you make me happy just by being you. Thank you for all the joy you give.

. . .

Happiness is a sunbeam. . . .
When it strikes a kindred heart,
like the converged lights upon a mirror,
it reflects itself with redoubled brightness.
It is not perfected until it is shared.

JANE PORTER

Happy Valentine's Day

Few delights can equal the mere presence
of one whom we trust utterly.

GEORGE MACDONALD

. . .

To love, and to be loved,
is the greatest happiness of existence.

SYDNEY SMITH

. . .

Love each other with genuine affection,
and take delight in honoring each other.

ROMANS 12:10 NLT

I am glad and share my joy with you. . . .
In the same way, you too must be glad
and share your joy with me.

PHILIPPIANS 2:17–18 TEV

. . .

*The greatest happiness of life is the conviction
that we are loved, loved for ourselves. . . .*

VICTOR HUGO

. . .

Like the sun, love radiates
and warms into life all that it touches.

O. S. MARDEN

When I'm sad and dreary, your love lights
my life with sunshine.

When I'm happy, your love makes life
seem even brighter.

When I'm lonely, your kindness comforts me.

When I'm proud, your love makes my
achievement shine even brighter.

When I'm discouraged, your belief in me helps me to go on.

When I'm upset and confused, your wise counsel helps me see my way more clearly.

Laughter shared is even more hilarious.

And in countless ways, your love helps me feel God's joyful presence within me.

Happy Valentine's Day

Love is the true means by which the world is enjoyed,
our love to others, and others' love to us.

THOMAS TRAHERNE

. . .

*Every time you smile at someone,
it is an action of love, a gift to that person,
a beautiful thing.*

MOTHER TERESA

. . .

Love is but the discovery of ourselves in others, and the
delight in the recognition.

ALEXANDER SMITH

Little acts of kindness which we render
to each other in everyday life,
are like flowers by the way-side to the traveler:
they serve to gladden the heart. . . .

EUNICE BATHRICK

. . .

*Y*ou have done so much to make my life happier and
more joyful. If each kind act of yours were a flower, my
hands would be overflowing with a bouquet of delight.
Thank you from the bottom of my heart for all the love
you show me.

Happy Valentine's Day

I thank God for all the happiness
He's given me through you.
May God give you as much joy
as you have given others.

. . .

Every time I think of you,
I give thanks to my God.
I always pray for you,
and I make my requests
with a heart full of joy.

PHILIPPIANS 1:3–4 NLT

Two

Love Means We're Never Alone

Love. . .binds everything together in perfect harmony.

COLOSSIANS 3:14 NRSV

Whenever I feel lonely, I think of you.
Just knowing that you love me, no matter what,
comforts my heart. Although we can't always be together,
you are still one of my life's dearest companions.
Thank you for always being there for me
whenever I need you.
I'm so glad I can count on your love.

No soul is desolate as long as there is a human being for whom it can feel trust and reverence.

GEORGE ELIOT

. . .

I cannot count the times I have been strengthened by another's heartfelt hug, appreciative note, surprise gift, or caring questions. . . .

DEE BRESTIN

. . .

Having someone who understands is a great blessing. . . .

JANETTE OKE

Happy Valentine's Day

The greatest gift is a portion of yourself.

RALPH WALDO EMERSON

. . .

Thank you for all the ways you give yourself to me.
Please know how much I appreciate all you've done.
Whenever I feel anxious or alone,
I'm comforted when I think of you.
I've always known I could count on you.
And in return,
please rely on me to be there when you need me.

. . .

I will very gladly spend for you everything I have and expend myself as well.

2 CORINTHIANS 12:15 NIV

Three

Love Is a Gift from God

Let us continue to love one another,
for love comes from God.
Anyone who loves is born of God and knows God.

1 JOHN 4:7 NLT

The love you've shown me is one of the best gifts God ever gave me. What would my life have been like without you? God has used you again and again to guide me, encourage me, and comfort me. I am so grateful He put you in my life.

. . .

We are the gift of the living God to one another.

REINE DUELL BETHANY

It is a gift of God to be able
to share our love with others.

MOTHER TERESA

. . .

*God himself has taught you
to love one another.*

1 THESSALONIANS 4:9 NLT

. . .

Love has its source in God,
for love is the very essence of His being.

KAY ARTHUR

Happy Valentine's Day

When we love each other God lives in us
and his love within us grows ever stronger.

1 JOHN 4:12 TLB

. . .

*When our relationships are born in the heart
of God, they bring out the best in us,
for they are nurtured by love.*

DON LESSIN

. . .

Your love for one another will prove to the world
that you are my disciples.

JOHN 13:35 NLT

Happy Valentine's Day

I prayed to God for courage. . .and He sent you to encourage me.

I asked God for comfort. . .and you brought His warmth to me.

I begged God to forgive me. . .and I felt His mercy through your forgiving spirit.

I doubted that God could really care for me. . . and you showed me that He did.

*N*o wonder then that I can't help but praise God for all that He has given me through you!

*E*ach of us needs a relationship with at least one
other person who also seeks and trusts the simple way,
the Simple Presence [of God].

TILDEN H. EDWARDS

. . .

*G*od bless the [one] who sees my needs
and reaches out a hand,
Who lifts me up, who prays for me,
and helps me understand.

AMANDA BRADLEY

. . .

*W*hen seeds of kindness are sown prayerfully in the
garden plot of our lives, we may be sure that there will
be a bountiful harvest of blessings for both us and others.

W. PHILLIP KELLER

*The secret of life is that all we have
and are is a gift of grace to be shared.*

LLOYD JOHN OGILVIE

. . .

God has shown me His grace through you.
When I felt as though no one understood me,
when I wondered if anyone could accept me,
when I believed that no one could love me,
you showed me your love.
God used your hands to touch my life.

Your heavenly Father knows your needs.
He will always give you all you need from day to day.

LUKE 12:30–31 TLB

. . .

God knew I needed you!
Thank you for your understanding heart.
Thank you for loving me.

. . .

A [relationship] in which heart speaks
to heart is a gift from God.

HENRY NOUWEN

Four

Love Is More Precious Than Gold, Sweeter Than Honey

Pleasant words are a honeycomb,
sweet to the soul and healing to the bones.

PROVERBS 16:24 NIV

Our world values possessions and money,
prestige and achievement.
But when it comes right down to it,
those things really matter very little.
Knowing you has taught me this: The sweetest,
most precious thing in all the world is the love
we show to one another.
Love is what makes our souls grow.

Only the heart knows how to find
what is precious.

FYODOR DOSTOYEVSKY

. . .

Love is not getting, but giving. . . .
It is goodness and honor and peace and pure living—yes,
love is that, and it is the best thing in the world
and the thing that lives the longest.

HENRY VANDYKE

. . .

A loving heart is the truest wisdom.

CHARLES DICKENS

In the presence of love—miracles happen!

ROBERT SCHULLER

. . .

Love is not blind; it is an extra eye,
which shows us what is
most worthy of regard.

JAMES MATTHEW BARRIE

. . .

We are all born for love.
It is the principle of existence and its only end.

BENJAMIN DISRAELI

Love is more valuable than. . .

* the biggest raise.
* the most expensive car.
* the grandest mansion.
* the finest jewelry.
* the most elaborate wardrobe.
* all the fame and fortune this world could
    ever offer.

Love is a debt which inclination always pays,
obligation never.

BLAISE PASCAL

. . .

Love accomplishes all things.

PETRARCH

. . .

Love sought is good,
but given unsought is better.

WILLIAM SHAKESPEARE

Happy Valentine's Day

We find rest in those we love,
and we provide a resting place in ourselves
for those who love us.

BERNARD OF CLAIRVAUX

. . .

Love is everything. It is the key of life,
and its influences are those that
move the world.

RALPH WALDO EMERSON

. . .

I'm so glad you are here. . . .
It helps me to realize how beautiful my world is.

RAINER MARIA RILKE

*A*fter all you've given me, I'm praying that in return God will send your heart a valentine of love. May you be filled to the brim with the richness and sweetness of His love.

. . .

"The LORD your God is with you. . . .
He will take great delight in you. . .
he will rejoice over you with singing."

ZEPHANIAH 3:17 NIV

Five

Love Is Eternal

Love. . .puts up with anything.
Trusts God always,
Always looks for the best,
Never looks back,
But keeps going to the end.
Love never dies.

1 CORINTHIANS 13:4, 7–8 THE MESSAGE

This world turns so fast that it's good to know some things never change. One of the things I count on in my life is your love. Although the years may alter us both in some ways, I know I can always rely on your love and understanding. Even death won't end the closeness we have shared.

And I'm looking forward to knowing you in heaven!

Happy Valentine's Day

Love remembers everything.

OVID

. . .

I will never forget the memories of love you've given me. Like treasured valentines, I will take them out year after year, lingering over them again, smiling as I remember all that you've done for me.

. . .

The heart hath its own memory, like the mind,
And in it are enshrined
The precious keepsakes, into which is wrought
The giver's loving thought.

LONGFELLOW

True friendships are lasting because true love is eternal.

HENRI NOUWEN

. . .

Love never gives up.
Love cares more for others than for self.
Love doesn't want what it doesn't have.

1 CORINTHIANS 13:4 THE MESSAGE

. . .

Though weary, love is not tired;
Though pressed, it is not straightened;
Though alarmed, it is not confounded.
Love securely passes through all.

THOMAS À KEMPIS

Happy Valentine's Day

No love. . .can cross the path of our destiny
without leaving some mark on it forever.

FRANCOIS MAURIAC

. . .

You have left your mark on my life,
and I am grateful.
I pray that someday I will be able
to give back to you a measure
of what you've given me.

. . .

Give away your life; you'll find life given back, but not
merely given back—given back with bonus and blessing.

LUKE 6:38 THE MESSAGE

*O*n Valentine's Day (and every day), I offer you a heart full of love. . .and a prayer that you will always know God's blessings.

. . .

May the Lord bless and protect you;
may the Lord's face radiate with joy because of you;
may he be gracious to you, show you his favor,
and give you his peace.

NUMBERS 6:24–26 TLB